DID YOU KNOW?
Frogs

DID YOU KNOW?

Frogs

Contents

What is a Frog?

- Frogs are **amphibians**. They are **cold-blooded** and reproduce by laying **eggs** that turn into **tadpoles** – but more of that later...

- They can **breathe** through their **lungs**, and also through their **skin** while under water. Tadpoles breathe through gills, just like a fish.

The amphibian family includes other groups such as newts.

- The closest relatives of Frogs include the **newts** and **salamanders**.
- **Toad** is a name given to some species of frogs, particularly those with **bumpy skin**. All toads are frogs.

Cane Toad.

Adult Golden Dart Frog.

Facts and figures

- There are more than **seven thousand** species of Frogs in the world today. They can be found on **every continent** except Antarctica.

- The greatest numbers of species live in **tropical regions** with, for example, more than **one thousand** species living in Brazil alone.

- Species such as the **Wood Frog** of North America and the **Common Frog** of Eurasia can survive in very cold conditions right up into the Arctic Circle.

Red-eyed Tree Frog lives in Central and South America.

Amazing adaptations

- Their **long legs** are perfect for swimming and also mean that many Frogs can jump more than **twenty times their body length** to help them escape from predators.
- Frogs have **webbed feet** that act like flippers to help them **swim faster.**

Frogs can jump long distances.

- Tree Frogs have **sticky toe pads** that help them to climb trees and other vertical surfaces.

Webbed feet with toe pads.

- **Protruding eyes** mean that a Frog can see above water while the rest of the animal remains hidden beneath the surface.

Protruding eye.

Big and small

• Some of the world's largest frogs include the **African Bullfrog** and **Goliath Frog** from Africa. These can weigh more than **three kilograms** and measure thirty centimetres from nose to 'tail' and **eighty centimetres** when including the extended legs.

The Red-banded Dart Frog measures about three centimetres.

African Bullfrog is one of the largest species.

- By contrast the **American Bullfrog** is a relative lightweight at a mere **fifteen centimetres** and **one kilogram**.
- Many of the famous colourful **Dart Frogs** from the Americas measure less than two centimetres.
- The world's smallest Frog species is the **Amau Frog** from New Guinea that measures less than **eight millimetres** when fully grown.

Amau Frog is the tiniest of all.

Weird and wonderful

- Many species of Frogs use **camouflage** to avoid their enemies – their **colours and patterns** help them to blend in perfectly with their backgrounds.

The bright colours of tiny Dart Frogs from Central and South America are a way of saying to potential predators: "I am toxic, don't eat me!"

Long-nosed Horned Frog (above) and Black Rain Frog (below).

- Other Frogs use a different strategy. They are **brightly coloured** in order to advertise to potential predators that they are **toxic** and not good to eat.
- Some species are very **unusual** and don't look much like Frogs at all. For example, the Long-nosed Horned Frog from South-East Asia the small-legged, beady-eyed Black Rain Frog from South Africa.
- The amazing Glass Frog from Central and South America has **transparent skin**.

The Vietnamese Mossy Frog takes camouflage to extremes.

The underside of a Glass Frog.

Frog lifecycle

- Frogs often use **calls** to attract a mate – these include croaking and high-pitched notes. Many species use inflatable air sacs to make the sound louder and carry for longer distances.
- Frogs lay **eggs**, usually in water – often these are clumps or strings of jelly-like **frogspawn**.

Adult frog with clumps of frogspawn.

Air sacs help to make a frog's calls louder.

- The eggs hatch into tiny **tadpoles**, which then grow bigger, develop legs and lose their tail as they grow into froglets. This process is called **metamorphosis**.
- A few frogs have **unusual breeding strategies**, such as **swallowing the eggs** so that they hatch inside the adult, or **brooding the eggs in a pouch**. Others lay their eggs in **a foam nest** attached to a plant.

The lifecycle progresses from egg to tadpole to froglet to adult frog.

Coping with extremes

● Despite being cold-blooded some Frogs are active in **freezing conditions** and will begin breeding in snow- and ice-covered pools. Some Frog species can even survive being **frozen solid** over the winter.

The urge to mate sees Frogs emerge in sub-zero temperatures in high mountains and arctic environments.

The Australian Common Spadefoot buries itself in mud during the dry season.

- Some species can **bury themselves in mud** and effectively **hibernate** for months at a time during the dry season until the rains come.

- Forests make excellent habitat for Frogs.

Many Tree Frog species are **adept climbers** that are able to get high off the ground into tree canopies to find food and shelter.

By climbing high into the canopy, Tree Frogs are able to make the most of the resources in their forest habitat.

- Most adult Frogs feed on insects such as **flies and beetles**, as well as other invertebrates such as **spiders and worms.**
- Many tadpoles are herbivores, feeding on **plants** and **algae.**

A tadpole's tiny mouth slurps up algae and small plants.

A wide mouth is useful for snapping up food.

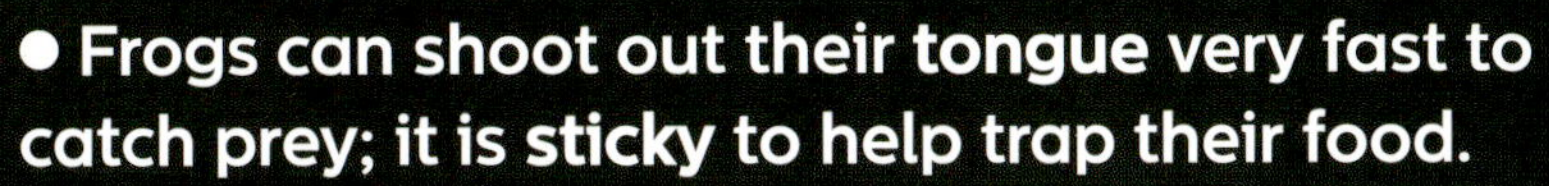

- Frogs can shoot out their **tongue** very fast to catch prey; it is **sticky** to help trap their food.
- They also have a **big, wide mouth** that helps them to snap up their bug prey.
- A Frog's **eyes** can be pushed down into its head to **help it swallow its food.**

Many Frogs use their long tongue to catch insect prey.

Threats to Frogs

- Habitat loss and pollution caused by humans are the main reasons that more than **one thousand five hundred** Frog species are classified as **Endangered** or **Critically Endangered** and threatened with Extinction.

- Frogs living in poor-quality environments altered by human activities are more likely to die from **deadly disease** caused by **chytrid fungus**. The fungus attacks their skin, which the Frogs use for breathing.

- Natural predators of Frogs include snakes and birds such as herons.

Snakes and herons among the predators of Frogs.

Many frog species around the world are Endangered, including the Southern Corroboree Frog of Australia.

By destroying habitat for development, humans are responsible for many threats to Frogs.

First published in 2026 by Young Reed
– an imprint of Reed New Holland

newhollandpublishers.com

A record of this book is held at the National Library of Australia.

ISBN 9781760798130

Other titles in the *'Did You Know?'* series:

Capybara
ISBN 9781760798048

Crocodiles
ISBN 9781760798116

Dolphins
ISBN 9781760798000

Kangaroos
ISBN 9781921073861

Koala
ISBN 9781921073878

Lizards
ISBN 9781921073885

Meerkat
ISBN 9781921073892

Monkeys
ISBN 9781760798031

Penguins
ISBN 9781921073908

Platypus
ISBN 9781760798161

Quokka
ISBN 9781760798109

Red Panda
ISBN 9781921073915

Rhinos
ISBN 9781760798123

Sharks
ISBN 9781921078017

Tasmanian Devil
ISBN 9781760798055

Tigers
ISBN 9781760798024

Kea
ISBN 9781760798062

Kiwi
ISBN 9781760798079

For details of these books and hundreds of other Natural History titles see newhollandpublishers.com

And keep up with Reed New Holland and New Holland Publishers on Facebook and Instagram
ReedNewHolland and NewHollandPublishers @ReedNewHolland and @NewHollandPublishers